EASY FINANCE FOR SMALL BUSINESSES

Sophie Wright

ISBN-13: 978-1517243876
ISBN-10: 1517243874

TABLE OF CONTENTS

INTRODUCTION

Setting up your own business is one of the most rewarding, thrilling and terrifying things a person can do. Approximately half of businesses fail in the early stages. It takes a good idea, a whole lot of perseverance and help and advice to succeed. A bit of luck helps too. I understand the pressures small businesses are under.

This guide is for entrepreneurs and small business owners who do not have the luxury of a Finance Director to advise them. I offer advice in areas that I feel are common pitfalls. My aim is to help your business succeed.

This guide is based on a series of blog posts which can be found at www.wrightcfoblog.wordpress.com. It is short and to the point, because as a business owner, time is a precious commodity.

"I can't imagine a person becoming a success who doesn't give this game of life everything he's got"- Walter Cronkite - CBS Journalist & Broadcaster

Chapter 1

SOLE TRADER VERSUS LIMITED COMPANY

You've made the brave decision to go ahead with your business idea and work for yourself. This is great news. It also means your to-do list is endless. One item that needs to be on your list, is choosing the right legal structure. This process can be daunting. I outline below, in basic straight forward terms what the options are and why you would want to choose one over the other. The good news is, if the one you've chosen does not turn out to be the right one for you, you are allowed to change it.

I am going to compare registering as a Sole Trader versus a Private Limited company as it pertains to the United Kingdom.

Sole trader- What is it?

• Classed as self-employed.

• You are allowed to have staff (just because you are a sole trader doesn't mean you have to do all the work yourself).

• You are personally responsible for the losses your business makes.

• In the same vein, you retain all profits of the business.

The paperwork

• Complete an annual self assessment tax return.

• Pay income tax on your profits.

• Pay national insurance.

• Register for VAT if takings are more than £82K a year.

Why choose this option?

• You are unsure about launching your idea and want to test the waters first without making too much of a big commitment. Remember, you can change type later.

• Lower accountancy fees and admin expenses.

• You have privacy. There is no need to declare to the world how much you are making, unlike a limited company.

Limited company- What is it?

• A Limited Company is registered at Companies House and has a corporate personality. It is a legal entity. It can be further divided into private and public, but if you are a start-up, I'm going to assume you are interested in 'private limited company' as an option and are not quite ready to go public. One step at a time!

• The company is responsible in its own right – business finances are separate to your personal finances.

• Profits are owned by the company after paying corporation tax.

• Company can share its profits.

• "Members" are people who own shares in the company.

• "Directors" are responsible for running the company.

• The legal responsibility of running the company lies with the directors.

The paperwork

• File annual statutory accounts (it is a criminal offence not to do so).

• Send Companies House an annual return.

• Send HMRC an annual company tax return.

• As above, you are required to be VAT registered if takings exceed £82K. See advice below re flat rate scheme.

• A director of the company needs to fill in a self

assessment tax return and pay any income tax and NI if paid a salary by the company.

Why choose this option?

The "limited" gives the company a bit more weight and appears to be bigger giving more confidence to potential investors, clients and suppliers.

Tax savings. Dividends of a limited company are subject to lower tax rates than self-employment income. (0% tax for basic rate tax payers and 10% for higher and additional rate tax payers). You can distribute dividends after 20% corp tax has been paid on profits.

Shareholders have no personal liability beyond the amount paid for the shares. If you do not succeed, and go bankrupt, it is the company that goes bankrupt, not you.

Raising finance. There is the option to raise funds by selling shares.

Top Tip

Although you don't have to register for VAT until you reach £82K income, you may want to register for it anyway. If you have very few purchases, for instance if you are a consultant, then you can register for the flat rate VAT scheme. Under this scheme, you cannot claim back VAT on purchases (who cares? You don't have any anyway) and although you can charge out 20% VAT you can pay back less to the government. Exact percentage depends on what your business sells exactly. Essentially, you get to keep some of the VAT.

Chapter 2

HOW TO WRITE A BUSINESS PLAN IN 4 HOURS

If you run your own business, no doubt you have had 'writing a business plan', on your to do list for some time. But who has time for that, when you are trying to get your business off the ground, right? Wrong. According to many sources, 90% of internet start-ups fail. You can lessen those odds by writing a plan. After all, "failing to plan is planning to fail".

This is why I have created an easy to follow summarised business plan, which you can do in four hours. If you need to raise capital or are asking a bank for a loan, you will need a more comprehensive plan. You can do that later. This will get you started and focused. It is also something you can share with suppliers, customers and potential partners who you'd like to invite come on board with you. So no more excuses.

Description

Write one paragraph, which answers these questions: Who are you? What do you do? Where do you do it?

The vision

What will this business be in five to ten years' time?

Brand promise

Write one paragraph. What will your company do for its clients?

Values

What are the core values that your business will stick to? Choose three and keep it short.

Objectives

Describe your business objectives. They should be long-term, e.g. in three years from now. They need to be SMART. (specific, measurable, achievable, realistic and timely) Choose three . (We only have four hours remember)

Market research

This can be two or three paragraphs but need to cover the following. What do you know about your industry? Who are your competitors? Who are your target customers? What is your unique selling point? What methods are you going to use to deliver your brand message.

Sales

How are you going to generate leads, get in front of customers and close the sale?

Housekeeping

This should be one or two paragraphs explaining the operations of the business. Include an organisational chart showing who is involved and where they are in the organisation.(No time to make a chart? Write a list instead) Include any business processes you may have. How are you going to measure quality satisfaction?

Financial plan

You should have three tables. 1. List of your start-up costs. 2. Revenue projections for three years. 3. Cashflow projections for three years. Have this as your basic plan and then build some sensitivity analysis around it. For instance, what happens if your revenue is off by 15%? What if it exceeds expectations by 15%? Use the basic budget as a base, and then have a best case and worst case scenario. The beauty of the worse case scenario, is that if your revenue is not what you think it should be, you know in advance, when you need to start adjusting your spend and if you don't, how long your money will last. It is your safety net and allows you to act quickly before it's too late.

Now, when I say you can do this in four hours, it's a bit like Jamie Oliver's meals in thirty minutes. Before Jamie starts his clock, his kettle is pre-boiled and his kitchen equipment is laid out on the counter before he even starts cooking. So get the kettle on, laptop is on charge, and you make sure you have no distractions. Don't answer email. Just sit down and write this plan. And in four hours, it will be done. You will feel so relieved to have crossed it off your list and you'll have a plan to get working towards. You will also have just increased your chances of business success.

Congratulations!

Chapter 3

CASHFLOW MANAGEMENT

There are countless reasons why businesses fail, such as choosing the wrong business partner, not listening to your customers or avoiding having a business website. But if you choose only one thing to get right, make sure it's your cash. 90% of small business failures are caused by poor cashflow, according to Dun & Bradstreet.

Here are my top 5 tips to having a healthy cashflow.

Create a cashflow forecast

A cashflow forecast is a planning tool which can be very simple to set up and maintain. I suggest creating a weekly one which spans up to 6 months. To create your cashflow, use a spreadsheet like excel, start with your current bank balance at the top. List all your outgoings for the week underneath it, and the income you expect to receive from clients. At the bottom, you should calculate what your expected cash balance should be by the end of the week. Teach someone in your organisation to keep this up to date and track its activity. You will be able to spot very quickly why things may be better or worse then you expected and you will know what you can afford to pay out. Set targets for your credit controller to ensure it is given enough attention and ownership.

Agreed terms & conditions

Have very clear payment terms which have been agreed upon by both parties before any work has begun. A clause in your client contract could say "Invoice will be supplied to Client once work is complete and Client will pay Company 30 days from the date of the invoice".. for example.

Agreement to these terms should be written or documented somewhere, in case anyone has sudden memory loss.

Invoice quickly

The sooner you get the invoice out the door, the quicker you will be paid. Devise a system whereby the person raising invoices is told exactly when a project is complete so that she or he can send the invoice out that day.

Have clear credit control procedures

These procedures should be documented and part of your credit controller's task list. Call your client's accounts payable department before the invoice is due to ensure it has landed in the right hands and there are no problems with it. I have seen invoice payments delayed by months because the addressee was wrong, or the wrong purchase order was used. Ask for a payment date and make a record of all calls to clients. If payment is late call again. Send statements once a month. Be a very polite and friendly pain in the neck.

Keep your friends close and your bank closer

It's a good idea to have a line of credit set up with your bank, just in case things don't go to plan. You want something to fall back on well before you actually need it.

Chapter 4

INCREASE PROFITS - 7 TIPS

There are some simple things you can do today, to start increasing your profits without winning new clients. Making some minor changes to the way you do business will be barely noticeable to anyone-apart from you, of course, as you'll know you are becoming more profitable.

Increase your prices. No really

A small increase in price will not drive your customers away. Even if it does drive some away, it will be a small number and you will still be better off with your remaining customers at the increased prices.

"Amazon raised its price of annual Prime Subscriptions from $79 to $99 in 2014. Despite the $20 increase, the company expected to lose less than 5% of customers, resulting in a hefty $400 million increase in income." John Boitnott, Oct 7, 2014

"In a McKinsey study with the Global 1200, they found that a 1% price increase – if the demand remained constant – would result on average in an 11% increase in profits. Not bad." Richard Ruff, Feb 9, 2015 Getting the picture?

Price alignment

Are you charging all your customers the same amount for similar products or services? Get everyone on the same price list or rate card. You may be charging some customers the same rate card you agreed when you signed the contract in 2005. Get up to speed.

Do not discount

Just as incremental price increases can increase your profit, so can the same incremental discounts be detrimental. Emphasize the value you bring. Not the price.

Cash discount from suppliers

If you are in a cash position where you can do so, it is better to get a discount to pay upfront, rather than pay full price and delay payment, even if you are borrowing. Just ask. They can only say no. And the chances are they won't ALL say no.

Check supplier bills

Do not assume that everyone invoices you correctly. Humans make mistakes. Are they overcharging you? Duplicating invoices? Do they add up? I have personally seen atrocious invoicing. Checking invoices from a film production company and questioning them once saved me (or rather the company I worked for at the time) £40K for one TV ad.

Same fixed costs, but cheaper

Check your running costs. Don't change what you're getting. Just pay less for it. There is a lot of competition out there for basic business supplies. For instance, everyone needs electricity. But are you paying the cheapest you can for it? There are companies out there who will analyze your usage and tell you what the best rate you can get is and from where. And it's free! The same goes with phone calls, broadband, even your stationery. Prices really differ from supplier to supplier for the exact same stationery.

Quotes for Capital Expenditure

For IT equipment, decide on a preferred supplier, which you promise to use as long as they always charge you 10% lower than if you bought directly from source. It works. I've done it. Their discount is more than yours so they still make a profit. Don't worry about them -worry about you. For any other big ticket item, never EVER buy anything unless you acquired three separate quotes. Make this a company rule.

Chapter 5

CLIENT PROFITABILITY- NOT ALL CLIENTS ARE CREATED EQUAL

Businesses are in the habit of measuring many things: customer satisfaction, financial performance, staff performance, market share and share value to name a few. And then there are hundreds of key performance indicators out there. David Parmenter has several books on the subject, in which he describes an endless number of them.

One of the most powerful things you can measure is client profitability. Because frankly, all clients are not created equal. There are various methods to conduct a CPA (Client Profitability Analysis) and it does depend on your industry. If you are a service business such as advertising, you will want to use time sheets to be able to know where your greatest assets (your staff) are spending their time. Or if you are in the business of conducting property inventories, then you need to identify all costs associated with a job, typing costs per report, time it takes per rooms in a property etc, in order to properly calculate your margins.

When I conduct a CPA, I investigate client income, associated labour and product costs and compare margins and growth opportunities between clients. The results are piled into a number crunching, sorting, filtering, moveable, living and breathing, data filled, excel spreadsheet. It's a beautiful thing. From here, the analysis begins.

Clients are then plotted onto a matrix. The results of which might clarify, for example, that Client A brings in a margin of 5%, but it brings in 50% of your revenue and Client B brings in a healthy margin of 25% but you only ever sold one item to them and they don't look like they want to return.

What's great about this analysis is your clients are categorised and according to that category, an appropriate strategy is allocated.

The result is a written report or presentation whereby your most and least profitable clients are revealed, not in terms of income, but margin and volume. It is a powerful analysis which often leads to a change in client strategy. Assess which clients, according to the analysis, you should aim to grow because they reap higher margins and which clients should be maintained with minimal effort or turned around, for example.

"A company can outperform rivals only if it can establish a difference that it can preserve. It must deliver greater value to customers or create comparable value at a lower cost, or do both" Michael Porter 1996. "What is Strategy", Harvard Business Review (Nov-Dec)

I have never conducted such an analysis, without management immediately making strategic changes to their business. If you want to grow your business, become more profitable and pose a bigger threat to your competition, a client profitability is a must. Without it, you are driving your business blind. Regain control.

Chapter 6

PRESSURE'S ON. HOW TO HANDLE THE RISE IN STAFF COSTS

On Sept 1st, 2015, average pay rises were to jump to 3.5% according to the DailyMail. Compulsory pension contributions are breathing down our necks. And the government has announced a rise in minimum wage from October 2015. All in all, staff costs are on the increase putting even more pressure on small businesses. 3.5% doesn't seem like much. So why should you care? You should care because it's a lot more money than you think it is.

Example

If you have a business with 20 employees, whose average annual salary is £45K plus 20% on-costs like national insurance and pension etc. An increase of 3.5% will cost you roughly £38K a year. Have you got this kind of money spare in your budget?

Keeping up with the current market

If you want to be an attractive company to work for and lure superb talent you need to pay market rate. You can find out if you are under or over paying your staff by looking at industry specific salary surveys.

If you are in the marketing communications industry for example and an IPA member, you can participate in their salary survey and receive the results. Not a member? You can gain similar information from Major Players.

Otherwise, you can access a salary guide from Reed or from Morgan McKinley. There are literally hundreds online. Let's assume you need to follow the trend and increase your employees' wages in order to stay competitive. Can't afford it? Don't panic. You have options.

One path is to increase other benefits besides actual pay. You can increase your employees' happiness, loyalty and productivity (because happy people are more productive – fact) at virtually no cost. There is an amazing list on Entrepreneur.com of low-cost perks. 'Bring your dog to work day. I know many people, male and female, personally who would be willing to take a small cut in pay if they knew their workplace offered work from home days and flexible hours to enable nursery pick up.

If you can not offer great wages, then offer quality of life and work life balance. These benefits rank higher on more people's agendas then you might think. And if they are provided with respect and trust, employees will repay you 10 fold.

Budget squeeze

Still need to squeeze out the extra pennies for pay rises? Here's how to find a little extra room.

Headcount assessment

What does everyone in your business do? Do you even know? Do they add value? Become a lean machine by discarding excess weight. Harsh perhaps, but necessary. "Life's tough kiddo" as my Dad used to day.

Subscriptions

How many pretty magazines sit in your reception never to be opened? What do they cost? Are they ALL necessary? And does every single director need their personal copy of the leading industry mag and the Financial Times? Smart companies have a rota. A small piece of paper with a list of names stapled to the front. Tick your name off when you've read it and pass it on. That's of course if you are still reading paper versions. Online subscriptions are better. Have a company login. One subscription which you share. Easy.

Example

You have 3 subscriptions to the FT for each of your directors. It's the full newspaper and online subscription at £13.50 a week. Switch to one shared basic online subscription at £5.35 a week and you have just saved £1,828 a year. Just share the company login. Now do it for all your publications. You can probably easily find £5K.

Switch to cheaper contracts

Switch your electricity and gas. You can use sites like Switch My Business or Energy Helpline . They find you the best deals for your area and your usage. You can save a substantial amount a year.

I suggest taking your overheads budget, and go down the list one by one. Ask yourself, what is this? Is it used? Do we need it? Can we get the same quality for less money?

If you have done all of the above, and you are still struggling to keep your head above water, then you need to take a hard long look at your revenue stream.

Chapter 7

SH*T HAPPENS. 5 KEY BUSINESS RISKS

We live in an unpredictable and volatile world. The only thing you can be certain about, is that life is uncertain. Be prepared. *"Aon (provider of risk management) says that 80% of companies that fail to recover from a major disaster will go out of business"*. Those are high odds which can be easily avoided if you have a plan. And it does not have to be complicated.

Here are my top 5 risks explained.

Business risks

These include increased competition and failure to innovate. Are you doing more of the same because it works for you right now? Your competitors are currently working on doing what you do, but better and cheaper. This is why you need to continually improve your product or service, keep up to date with technological advances and know what your competitors are up to. Don't keep up – get ahead. If you have the luxury of being able to afford a new business development person, great. If not, then you've just added something else onto your job spec. Don't be a Kodak.

Reputation risks

"It takes 20 years to build a reputation and five

minutes to ruin it. If you think about that, you'll do things differently." -Warren Buffet.

If something happens, a failure in some way, a dent in your rep, act immediately. Do not ignore it; NEVER let it fester.   It will snowball into a mountain of unpleasantness. Call a board meeting, agree on a PR message which tackles the issue and get the message out ASAP.

Theft

In my experience it is not usually worth insuring company mobile phones against theft, but IT equipment insurance is essential and always outweighs the costs. Risk is easily mitigated. CCTV cameras are extremely useful in revealing the source of any thefts, (as well as finding out if anyone secretly sleeps in the office!). The very sign on the wall showing there is a camera acts as a great deterrent.   Other forms of theft I have encountered over the years include misuse of company credit cards. Someone should always sign off expenses and check credit card receipts. No matter what level they are. Make it policy and lead by example.

Data Protection

You are legally obliged to protect personal information about your clients, suppliers and employees. Don't get caught out- know the rules. The Information Commissioner's Office (ICO)'s website is a wonderful resource.

https://ico.org.uk/for-organisations/guide-to-data-protection/

You can find advice and guidelines for direct marketing, holding customer information, a checklist for small businesses and much more. If you fail to keep up with the law you are at risk of being fined up to £500,000. Ouch.

IT risks

A tornado, an earthquake or a comet pays you a visit. It's all gone: client list, accounts, creative work, all of it. You're on the cloud right? If properly set up, you should able to access everything from your safe location. IT risk management can of course get a lot more complicated than this. But if you are small business starting up, I suggest choosing an accounts system and a server system which are cloud based. It's a good start.

It goes without saying, make sure you are properly insured for fire, terrorism, employers' liability, director and officers insurance, professional indemnity, public liability. You can get a bundle business package which covers it all.

Chapter 8

HOW TO BOOST THE VALUE OF YOUR COMPANY

If you are thinking of selling your business one day, even if it is in 5 years' time, you need to begin boosting the sale value today. If and when you finally sell, your buyers, their lawyers, consultants and accountants, will all be looking through your company's past history... in extreme detail. Possibly for the previous 5 years.

Here's what you can do now to make sure you get highest price for the sale of your business.

Growth

Steady, financial growth is essential. Have a clear written down plan on how fast the business will grow, and how you are going to achieve it. When your buyer's representatives are unpicking your year on year financial statements, they will be looking for anything that can lower the sale price. If your accounts reveal nice and steady revenue and net profit growth, you're singing.

Profits

Very few people are going to buy your business, or at least at a good price, if you are not even making a profit. Do everything in your power to make a profit, and then increase it year on year. Increase your revenues be it through expanding existing clients, or by winning new business, increase efficiencies and eliminate waste. Is work being duplicated? Are costs being duplicated? Do everything you can to maximise this. A common way to value a company is to take their post-tax profits and times it by a number- let's say 5 for example. In this scenario, if you increase your profit by £100, it has increased your sale value by £500. Every pound counts.

No skeletons

Skeletons in the financial closet= price slashing. Have procedures and processes for most things, in particular everything financially related. Have a folder for company policies which can be easily reached. They should include things like capital expenditure and sign off policy, expenses policies, credit control procedures- all the basics. Your balance sheet accounts should be reconciled monthly when you close your books for the month. This may sound standard for many, but so many small companies wait until the end of year only to find a whole heap of surprises. Do you know what's in your balance sheet? Be over-the-top. Spring clean your accounts.

Contracts

Ensure your clients have contracts. They should include payment terms, what work is included and what would be additional cost, termination clauses and insurance coverage including who is accountable for what. If appropriate include IP rights. Ensure all your employees have employment agreements too. These should include anti-competitor clauses, especially for senior staff. When you sell a business, there is a risk that clients will go with their account holders should they leave, and not stay with the company. Mitigate this risk, (and avoid the risk being cause for devaluing sale price) by putting in this clause.

Succession planning

It's all about reducing risk. When you sell, the chances are once the earn-out is finished, you will be moving on to your next venture. Who will take your place? Your buyers need to feel confident that business will resume as normal and that there is a plan. Hire your successors now. Train them, mentor them, be sure they are ready when the time comes. And that they want it!

Team

What about the rest of the team that make up your company? Every single employee makes your business what it is. Make sure you have good, loyal, high quality staff who are happy and committed. They, after all, are what your buyers are buying.

For more information in regards to when to sell your company, how to sell or choosing the right advisor, B Gateway have some good tips here. http://www.bgateway.com/

If you are an advertising agency and specifically desire to sell your company to WPP, Peter Levitan has a good article about what to consider.

http://peterlevitan.com/8-tips-for-how-to-sell-your-ad-agency-5744/

About The Author

Sophie Wright is owner of WrightCFO Ltd and a Finance Director Consultant. She advises small to medium sized businesses who are either getting off the ground, entering a new stage of growth, or looking for some financial insight.

Born and raised in Canada, Sophie has been residing in the UK for the last 17 years, where she has been working in the marketing and advertising, digital media and technology sectors.

Sophie is a member of the Chartered Institute of Management Accountants, the Association of Accounting Technicians and has a Bachelor of Arts in philosophy and sociology.

For a free consultation please contact Sophie Wright directly.

Email: sophie@wrightcfo.co.uk
Website: www.wrightcfo.co.uk
Blog: www.wrightcfoblog.wordpress.com
Twitter: @sophielwight
LinkedIn:
https://uk.linkedin.com/in/sophiewright